W9-BJS-640

EDGE
BOOKS™

Epic Disasters

THE WORST EARTHQUAKES OF ALL TIME

by Mary Englar

Consultant:
Susan L. Cutter, PhD
Director
Hazards and Vulnerability Research Institute
University of South Carolina

Edge Books are published by Capstone Press,
1710 Roe Crest Drive, North Mankato, Minnesota 56003.
www.capstonepub.com

Books published by Capstone Press are manufactured with paper
containing at least 10 percent post-consumer waste.

Library of Congress Cataloging-in-Publication Data
Englar, Mary.
  The worst earthquakes of all time / by Mary Englar.
      p. cm.—(Edge books. epic disasters)
  Includes bibliographical references and index.
  Summary: "Describes the worst earthquakes in history, as well as formation, scale,
and disaster tips"—Provided by publisher.
  ISBN 978-1-4296-7657-1 (library binding)
  ISBN 978-1-4296-8013-4 (paperback)
  1. Earthquakes—History—Juvenile literature. I. Title. II. Series
  QE521.3.E54 2012
  363.34'9509—dc23   2011037979

Editorial Credits

Anthony Wacholtz, editor; Veronica Correia, designer; Marcie Spence,
      media researcher; Laura Manthe, production specialist

Photo Credits

AP Images: Anjum Naveed, 21, Dita Alangkara, 18, Imaginechina, 17, Library of
Congress, 14, Matt Marek/American Red Cross, 6; Corbis: Bettmann, 9, 25, 27,
Sergio Dorantes/Sygma, 13; Getty Images: David McNew, 29, Pierre Verdy/AFP, 22;
Shutterstock: fotosav, cover, 1, Lee Prince, 5, upstudio, cover (top left)

Printed in the United States of America in North Mankato, Minnesota.
122012   007098R

TABLE OF CONTENTS

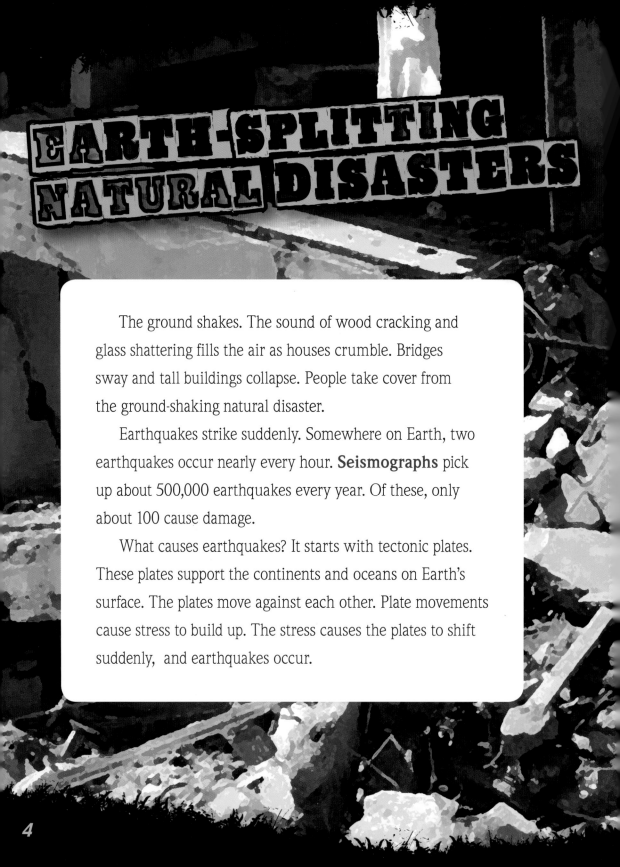

EARTH-SPLITTING NATURAL DISASTERS

The ground shakes. The sound of wood cracking and glass shattering fills the air as houses crumble. Bridges sway and tall buildings collapse. People take cover from the ground-shaking natural disaster.

Earthquakes strike suddenly. Somewhere on Earth, two earthquakes occur nearly every hour. **Seismographs** pick up about 500,000 earthquakes every year. Of these, only about 100 cause damage.

What causes earthquakes? It starts with tectonic plates. These plates support the continents and oceans on Earth's surface. The plates move against each other. Plate movements cause stress to build up. The stress causes the plates to shift suddenly, and earthquakes occur.

THE RICHTER SCALE

Many scientists use the Richter scale to measure the magnitude of earthquakes. Weak earthquakes are given a low magnitude. Powerful earthquakes are rated 7 or higher.

MAGNITUDE   POSSIBLE EFFECTS

1...................... detectable only by instruments

2...................... barely detectable

3...................... felt indoors

4...................... slight damage

5...................... minor to moderate damage

6...................... moderate destruction

7...................... serious damage

8...................... devastating damage

seismograph—a machine used to detect and record ground motion caused by earthquakes
magnitude—a measure of the size of an earthquake

TROUBLE IN HAITI

DATE: January 12, 2010
LOCATION: Port-au-Prince, Haiti
MAGNITUDE: 7.0

FACT:

The Presidential Palace in Port-au-Prince that was completed in 1920 was destroyed in the 2010 earthquake.

The island nation of Haiti is one of the poorest countries in the world. Port-au-Prince, the crowded capital city, is home to more than 2 million people. Haiti wasn't prepared for a major earthquake. The city had very poor construction of its buildings and houses.

On January 12, 2010, an earthquake hit Port-au-Prince at 4:53 p.m. The earthquake's **epicenter** was a few miles southwest of the capital. Schools, government buildings, and hospitals collapsed. People ran into the streets to escape from the falling buildings. Chunks of concrete from the collapsed buildings blocked roads. Emergency workers could not reach many survivors. There was no heavy equipment available to clear the roads.

After the earthquake, a cloud of dust and smoke covered the city. People huddled in open spaces as evening fell. There was no power, water, or phone networks. People could not get in touch with their family or friends.

The magnitude 7.0 quake wasn't the strongest of the year, but it hit in one of the poorest places in the world. It killed more than 200,000 people and left hundreds of thousands of survivors living in tents.

epicenter—the point on Earth's surface directly above the place where an earthquake occurs

DATE: May 22, 1960
LOCATION: Chile
MAGNITUDE: 9.5

Earthquakes with a 7.0 magnitude or higher are rare. On average, 16 occur each year. Of those, only one reaches an 8.0 magnitude. But in 1960, Chile experienced the strongest earthquake ever recorded—a 9.5 magnitude quake.

Chile lies along the southwestern coast of South America. A **fault** lies off the coast of Chile. The fault is where the Nazca tectonic plate meets the South American tectonic plate. The Nazca plate pushes beneath the South American plate, causing earthquakes.

On May 21, 1960, many towns along Chile's central coast experienced four strong earthquakes. The quakes caused severe damage to homes and businesses. On May 22, the 9.5 earthquake occurred. After the ground stopped shaking, three large **tsunamis** slammed into the coast. The waves caused more destruction than the earthquake. About 1,600 people were killed in the disasters.

fault—a crack in the earth where two plates meet; earthquakes often occur along faults

tsunami—a large, destructive ocean wave caused by an underwater earthquake, landslide, or volcanic eruption

THE DEADLIEST EARTHQUAKE IN HISTORY

DATE: January 23, 1556
LOCATION: Shaanxi (Shensi), China
MAGNITUDE: estimated 8.0

At the top of the list of the world's worst earthquakes is the 1556 quake that hit the Shaanxi province in China. The earthquake claimed the lives of more than 830,000 people— at least 500,000 more than the 2010 Haiti earthquake.

Several factors, including **liquefaction**, caused most of the buildings to collapse. The soil underneath the buildings was moist and loosely packed. The earthquake caused the soil to act like a liquid. Without sturdy ground under the foundations, the buildings toppled.

The earthquake changed the land, creating even more problems. Mountains collapsed. Paths of several rivers changed. Many provinces experienced major flooding.

liquefaction—the process of soil becoming fluidlike and unstable during an earthquake

After the earthquake, it was clear changes needed to be made. Wood and bamboo replaced the stone used to construct the buildings. The wooden and bamboo buildings were softer and more resistant to earthquakes.

1556 SHAANXI EARTHQUAKE

○ approximate epicenter

Shaanxi province

provinces affected

SHAKY GROUND

DATE: September 19, 1985
LOCATION: Mexico City, Mexico
MAGNITUDE: 8.0

Earthquakes can become more deadly depending on where they hit. When an earthquake hit Mexico City on September 19, 1985, the soft, moist soil made the disaster worse. The soft soil increased the power of the **seismic waves** that sped through the ground. The unsteady buildings toppled quickly.

The magnitude 8.0 quake hit at 7:18 a.m. about 200 miles (322 kilometers) west of Mexico City. Thousands of buildings in the capital were damaged or destroyed. At least 100,000 people lost their homes. Telephone lines were cut off. People could smell gas in the streets and worried that fires might break out.

Many people were rescued from the collapsed buildings. Rescue workers saved 58 babies found in a hospital three days later. But the death toll was still high. At least 9,500 people died. After the earthquake, the Mexican government passed laws to make new buildings stronger.

seismic wave—a wave created by an earthquake

FACT:

The Spanish defeated the Aztecs in 1521. After their victory, they filled in Lake Texcoco to have more land for their new city. Today downtown Mexico City is built on the remains of the lake.

THE SAN FRANCISCO EARTHQUAKE OF 1906

DATE: April 18, 1906

LOCATION: San Francisco, California

MAGNITUDE: 7.8

An earthquake can be deadly on its own. But it can also trigger other destructive events, such as mudslides and tsunamis. In San Francisco in 1906, a powerful earthquake caused an outbreak of fires that destroyed most of the city.

Early on the morning of April 18, 1906, a magnitude 7.8 earthquake struck San Francisco. The minute-long quake knocked down houses and bent train tracks.

Soon after the quake, fires broke out in the business district. Firefighters did not have enough water to put out the flames. The earthquake had broken water mains and pipelines. As the fires burned for the next two days, the army tried to stop the blaze with dynamite. They hoped to create a **firebreak** between buildings, but it didn't work. In fact, the dynamite blast may have created more fires. By the time the fires went out, the disaster had claimed about 3,000 lives.

THE SAN ANDREAS FAULT

San Francisco lies near the San Andreas Fault. On April 18, 1906, about 267 miles (430 km) along the San Andreas Fault showed signs of ground movement. In one place, two pieces of a fence moved about 15 feet (5 meters) apart.

firebreak—an area cleared by firefighters to stop fires from spreading

HIGH IN THE MOUNTAINS

DATE: May 12, 2008
LOCATION: Sichuan province, China
MAGNITUDE: 7.9

China has a long history of earthquakes. Because some cities are located high in the mountains, the shaking ground can have a deadly impact.

On May 12, 2008, a 7.9-magnitude earthquake hit the mountains of Sichuan province. Many villages and cities in the mountains and along river valleys were affected. The severe shaking caused landslides. The landslides blocked the narrow mountain roads. Some survivors hiked many hours down the mountains to find shelter and food.

The Chinese army rushed soldiers out to help with search and rescue. However, huge boulders blocked the roads. The soldiers were unable to take their trucks and supplies into the damaged areas. The army eventually sent helicopters in to rescue survivors and drop off supplies.

More than 87,000 people died or went missing in the 2008 quake. Many of them were children. It was the deadliest earthquake in China in 30 years.

DAMS FROM LANDSLIDES

The landslides created another problem for the survivors. Mud and debris from the landslides blocked some rivers completely. More than 30 lakes formed behind these dams. The largest lake threatened more than 1 million people downstream. Government engineers and soldiers blasted through tons of rock to release the water safely.

POWERFUL EARTHQUAKE, DEADLY TSUNAMI

DATE: December 26, 2004
LOCATION: Sumatra, Indonesia
MAGNITUDE: 9.1

Around 8:00 a.m. on December 26, 2004, a powerful earthquake shook the west coast of northern Sumatra, Indonesia. Building pressure between two plates was forcefully released. The result was a rift in the earth more than 600 miles (966 km) long. The earthquake hit 9.1 on the Richter scale. It was the third-largest recorded earthquake in the world.

Within three days of the earthquake, powerful **aftershocks** hit the area. A 7.1 aftershock occurred three hours after the earthquake. Thirteen of the aftershocks had at least a 6.0 magnitude.

KILLER TSUNAMI

The Sumatra earthquake was just the beginning. The earthquake created a tsunami in the Indian Ocean. The tsunami traveled about 3,000 miles (4,828 km). It was 50 feet (15 m) high in some places when it slammed into 11 countries along the Indian Ocean. More than 220,000 people were killed or went missing.

aftershock—a smaller earthquake that follows a large one

BRIEF BUT DEADLY

DATE: October 8, 2005
LOCATION: Pakistan
MAGNITUDE: 7.6

Millions of years ago, the Indian tectonic plate crashed into the Eurasian tectonic plate. The collision gradually created the towering mountains in northern Pakistan and India. Today pressure from the plates causes many earthquakes.

On October 8, 2005, a magnitude 7.6 earthquake struck 65 miles (105 km) north of Pakistan's capital city of Islamabad. The epicenter was in the mountains. The quake set off landslides that blocked roads into the most damaged areas.

Pakistan's army worked to clear the roads, but it took several days to reach many mountain villages. Helicopters flew in soldiers, water, and food. They picked up injured people and flew them to hospitals. More than 86,000 people died. Millions were forced to live in tents during the cold winter.

QUAKE IN THE NIGHT

DATE: August 17, 1999
LOCATION: northwestern Turkey
MAGNITUDE: 7.6

At around 3:00 a.m. on August 17, 1999, most people in Izmit, Turkey, were sleeping. But their peaceful sleep was quickly interrupted. The heavily populated city was awakened by a strong 7.6-magnitude earthquake. The epicenter was about 7 miles (11 km) from Izmit in the Kocaeli province.

Turkey had experienced several powerful earthquakes in the past. In the previous 60 years, 17 earthquakes of 6.7 magnitude or higher had shaken the country. Still, many of the buildings were not built to survive an earthquake. They could not withstand the intense shaking of the powerful 1999 quake.

Because so many people lived in the region, the death toll was especially high. At least 17,000 people were killed and about 50,000 were injured. About 500,000 people were left without homes.

THE NORTH ANATOLIAN FAULT

The 1999 Turkey earthquake occurred on one of the world's most-studied faults, the North Anatolian Fault. Maps of the area show the North Anatolian Fault is similar to the San Andreas Fault. Scientists from the United States and Turkey have worked together to learn more about the two similar faults.

THE GOOD FRIDAY EARTHQUAKE

DATE: March 27, 1964
LOCATION: Prince William Sound, Alaska
MAGNITUDE: 9.2

It was the Friday before Easter in 1964. Most kids had the day off from school. Many businesses were also closed, so most people were at home.

The quiet evening was interrupted by a powerful earthquake. At 5:36 p.m., the first shock occurred. The ground shook for nearly three minutes. The earthquake damaged many towns along the Alaskan coast. Docks fell into the sea, railroad tracks bent and twisted, and many buildings collapsed. The 9.2-magnitude earthquake was the strongest earthquake in North America and the second strongest in the world. Only the 1960 Chile quake was more powerful.

After the quake, a tsunami hit the coastal towns in Alaska. The giant wave also reached Hawaii, Canada, and the west coast of the United States. While only 15 people died in the earthquake, the tsunami claimed 113 lives.

FACT:

As many as 4,000 earthquakes occur in Alaska each year. Most of them are too weak to be noticed without instruments.

DISASTERS IN JAPAN

DATE: September 1, 1923 and March 11, 2011
LOCATION: Japan
MAGNITUDE: 7.9 and 9.0

On a quiet Saturday in 1923, most shops and businesses in Tokyo, Japan, were closing for the weekend. Many families gathered at home for lunch. Just before noon, a magnitude 7.9 earthquake struck about 50 miles (80 km) south of Tokyo. An American visiting Japan described what he saw. "The houses, most of them two-storied, frail wooden structures with paper windows … had been torn apart." About two-thirds of Tokyo's buildings burned to the ground.

Many Japanese cooked on coal stoves, and the hot coals spilled during the earthquake. Fires broke out and spread quickly to other cities. Firefighters had lost much of their equipment in the quake and the water mains were broken. The fire burned out of control into the night. The Tokyo-Yokohama area of the Kanto region was hit the hardest. More than 140,000 people in that area died from the powerful quake and fire.

About 90 years later, a 9.0-magnitude earthquake shook Honshu, Japan, on March 11, 2011. But it was only one of several disasters that day. The earthquake triggered a tsunami reaching more than 100 feet (30 m). The tsunami flooded a nuclear power plant on the coast. The plant lost electricity, which was used to run the cooling pumps inside the reactors. The reactors overheated, causing a meltdown. People were evacuated from the area. The threat of radiation delayed the rescue and medical care of survivors. More than 15,000 people were killed from the combined disasters.

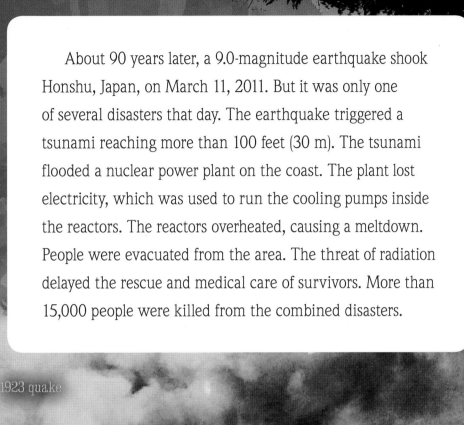

1923 quake

FACT:
Nearly 90 percent of the world's earthquakes and volcanic eruptions occur in a zone around the Pacific plate in the Pacific Ocean. The area is known as the Pacific Ring of Fire.

LIVING WITH EARTHQUAKES

Earthquakes can be deadly. It's important for you and your family to be prepared if an earthquake strikes. Each family member should know what to do if an earthquake hits. If you're indoors, you should drop to the floor and take shelter under a heavy, sturdy piece of furniture. Hold onto the furniture to try to keep it from moving away during the shaking. Stay away from windows. Telephones may not work, so make sure your family has a backup plan for how to communicate after an earthquake.

If you're outside when an earthquake hits, stay in an open space away from buildings. Don't try to run inside a building—it might collapse as you run into it. Stay away from electrical wires and street lights that might fall.

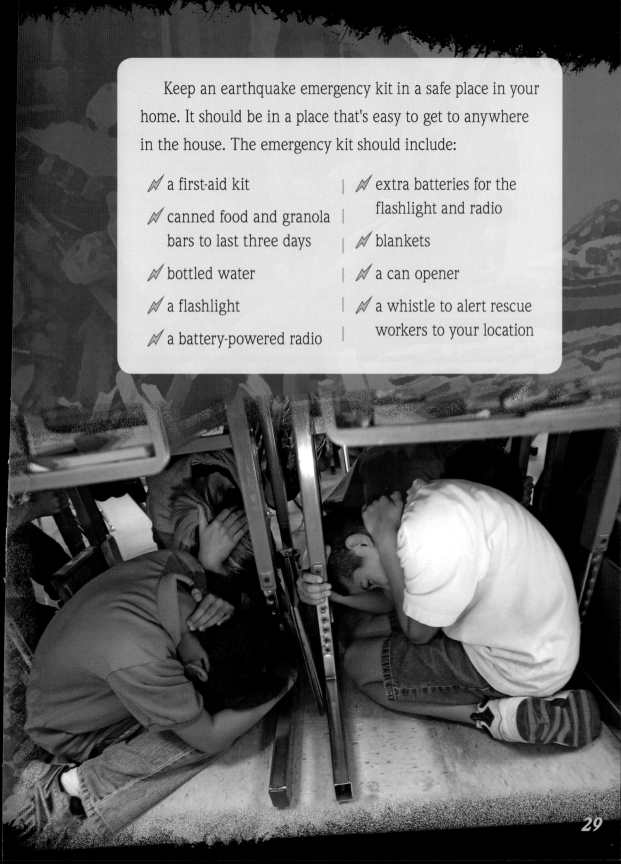

Keep an earthquake emergency kit in a safe place in your home. It should be in a place that's easy to get to anywhere in the house. The emergency kit should include:

- a first-aid kit
- canned food and granola bars to last three days
- bottled water
- a flashlight
- a battery-powered radio

- extra batteries for the flashlight and radio
- blankets
- a can opener
- a whistle to alert rescue workers to your location

GLOSSARY

aftershock (AF-tur-shok)—a smaller earthquake that follows a large one

debris (duh-BREE)—the scattered pieces of something that has been broken or destroyed

epicenter (EP-uh-sent-ur)—the point on Earth's surface directly above the place where an earthquake occurs

fault (FAWLT)—a crack in the earth where two plates meet; earthquakes often occur along faults

firebreak (FIRE-brayk)—an area cleared by firefighters to stop fires from spreading

liquefaction (lik-wuh-FAC-shun)—the process of soil becoming fluidlike and unstable during an earthquake

magnitude (MAG-nuh-tood)—a measure of the size of an earthquake

radiation (ray-dee-AY-shuhn)—tiny particles sent out from radioactive material

Richter scale (RIK-tur SKALE)—a scale that measures the amount of energy in an earthquake; 1 is the weakest, and 10 is the strongest

Ring of Fire (RING UHV FIRE)—an area of seismic activity that circles around the Pacific Ocean; the Ring of Fire is known for earthquakes and volcanic activity

seismic wave (SIZE-mik WAYV)—a wave created by an earthquake

seismograph (SIZE-muh-graf)— a machine used to detect and record ground motion caused by earthquakes

tectonic plate (tek-TAHN-ik PLAYT)—a section of Earth's crust that supports continents and oceans

tsunami (tsoo-NAH-mee)—a large, destructive ocean wave caused by an underwater earthquake, landslide, or volcanic eruption

READ MORE

Griffey, Harriet. *Earthquakes and Other Natural Disasters.* DK Readers. New York: Dorling Kindersley, 2010.

Montgomery, Heather. *How to Survive an Earthquake.* Prepare to Survive. Mankato, Minn.: Capstone Press, 2009.

Reingold, Adam. *Leveled by an Earthquake!* Disaster Survivors. New York: Bearport Pub., 2010.

Walker, Sally M. *Earthquakes.* Early Bird Earth Science. Minneapolis: Lerner Publications, 2008.

INTERNET SITES

FactHound offers a safe, fun way to find Internet sites related to this book. All of the sites on FactHound have been researched by our staff.

Here's all you do:

Visit *www.facthound.com*

Type in this code: 9781429676571

Super-cool stuff! Check out projects, games and lots more at
www.capstonekids.com

INDEX